I would, but my
DAMN MIND
won't let me

I would, but my DAMN MIND won't let me

A Guide for Teen Girls:
How to Understand and Control Your
Thoughts and Feelings

Book 2 of 3
Words of Wisdom for Teens Series

Jacqui Letran

DUNEDIN, FLORIDA

First edition: © February 2015 by Jacqui Letran.

Second edition: © September 2016 by Jacqui Letran.

Publisher's Cataloging-In-Publication Data

(Prepared by The Donohue Group, Inc.)

Names: Letran, Jacqui.
Title: I would, but my damn mind won't let me: a teen's guide to
    controlling their thoughts and feelings / Jacqui Letran.
Description: 2nd edition. | Asheville, North Carolina: A Healed
    Mind, [2016] | Series: Words of wisdom for teens series; book
    2 | Interest age level: 12 and up.
Identifiers: ISBN 978-0997624403 | ISBN 978-0-9976244-1-0 (e-
book)
Subjects: LCSH: Adolescent psychology. | Teenagers--Attitudes. |
    Happiness in adolescence. | Emotions in adolescence. | Self-
    help techniques for teenagers.
Classification: LCC BF724 .L48 2016 (print) | LCC BF724 (e-
    book) | DDC 155.5--dc2

Praise for Jacqui Letran's

*I would, but my **DAMN MIND** won't let me*
a Guide for Teen girls to Understand and Control Your
Thoughts and Feelings

"Letran helps readers understand how the mind can often send confusing (and sometimes detrimental) signals as a means of protecting one's-self from pain. The author breaks down the root causes of many mental obstacles which can often seem insurmountable while providing solutions for long-term stability and happiness. Topics such as fear and self-doubt are addressed in a way which is profound in its simplicity. This book will appeal to readers of all ages and genders. *I would, but my Damn Mind won't let me!* is highly recommended for home, school and public libraries and for use in clinical settings." **Literary Classics Lumen Award Winner, 2016**

"Jacqui Letran's self-help guide for young adults is an engrossing and highly accessible guide for anyone who'd like to understand why they react to stress and stressors the way they do. I was impressed by the way the author introduces the complex and complicated processes that go on in the human mind and especially appreciated how she's adapted her findings and techniques to work with young women. Her case studies were fascinating and clearly demonstrated how depression and other mental health issues can sometimes be resolved without the use of medicines and traditional therapeutic methods. This is a well-written and informative work that is neither condescending nor patronizing of its target audience, and it is highly recommended." **Readers' Favorite Gold Medal Award Winner, 2016**

"All teenagers should read this book as it is helpful in guiding them to eliminate the baggage they are carrying inside. Jacqui Letran's writing style is simple and easy to understand. I recommend this book to all teenagers who are experiencing low self-esteem, anxiety, stress, and want to improve themselves. The book is not only for teenagers, but is also helpful for adults as well." **Mamta Madhavan, reviewer for Readers Favorite**

Self-help textbooks for adolescents may inundate the literary marketplace, but this outstanding title surpasses the majority in its creative yet uncomplicated presentation of life-altering advice. A winner stands behind this valuable toolbox, a gleaming treasure chest for anyone who needs a psychological boost. **The BookLife Prize. Quarter Finalist**

"I just finished reading, *I would, but my Damn Mind won't let me!* by Jacqui Letran and this book needs to be on every teen girl's bookshelf (only after her parents have read it first!) Jacqui uses teen-friendly language, analogies and real-life portrayals to engage with and speak directly to a teen girl's struggles. She teaches in an easy to understand way how your daughter's mind creates thoughts, feelings and beliefs at an early age that may no longer serve her as she grows up. Your daughter will learn specific how-to's for identifying limiting beliefs, so she can clear the way to confidence, self-compassion and loving who she is!" **Kim Restivo, MA, Pediatric Psychotherapist**

Table of Contents

Dedication

This book is dedicated to all the teens out there who are struggling with insecurities, self-doubts, or self-sabotaging thoughts and actions. Even though you may not believe it yet, please borrow my certainty that you have everything you need within yourself to overcome your struggles. I believe in you. I know that you can make significant positive changes in your life by understanding and controlling your mind. Read this book with an open mind and a willingness to try something different and get ready to be amazed by the results you'll find.

CHAPTER 1

Why Can't You Just Control Yourself?

How many times have you been told by well-meaning parents, adults, or even your friends that you should just stop thinking or feeling a certain way? They tell you that the problems you have are all in your head. They tell you to stop making a big deal out of things, that you're too sensitive, and there is no reason to be nervous or anxious.

And yet, you are. You don't know what to think or how to feel. You feel tense and nervous. Others seem to have it so easy. But for you, life is difficult and so unfair!

Your situation may seem hopeless; perhaps you have even concluded that you were just "born that way" and there is nothing you can do to change.

But what if you are wrong about that conclusion? What if there was a way for you to create the changes you desperately desire? What if I can teach you how to take control of your mind, thoughts, and feelings? Would you want to learn how to do that for yourself?

The power of the human mind is incredible. It is capable of creating horrible life experiences, and it is capable of creating happy, successful ones, too. It might not feel that way right now, but you do get to choose which life experiences you'll have.

Once you learn easy, yet highly effective ways to take charge of your mind, you'll find that you have the power to create the life you want and deserve. The power to create permanent, positive change is available to you no matter what you are struggling with.

Stop wasting your energy and time on those old, useless emotions and thoughts. Today is the day to change your life experiences.

This book will show you how to:
- Challenge your old negative belief patterns
- Stop unhealthy thoughts and feelings
- Create positive life experiences for yourself
- Stay calm and in control in any situation
- Unleash the power of your mind to create the life you want and deserve

Everyone's journey to happiness begins with the belief that happiness is possible. Even if your personal experiences have led you to believe you will have a difficult life filled with stress, anxiety, and unhappiness, I will show you that you do have other options. You can learn to believe that happiness is possible for you.

In this book, I will show you how to take charge of your mind to overcome your obstacles and struggles. I will show you simple, yet powerful principles to strengthen your self-belief that leads to a solid foundation for happiness and success.

The next time somebody asks you, "Why can't you just control yourself?" you can smile and thank them for the gentle reminder and instantly take control of your thoughts and feelings again.

You are the key to your success and happiness.

Close your eyes and imagine for a moment how wonderful your life will be once you fully understand how to control your thoughts, feelings, and actions. If you are ready to make that dream-life your reality, I encourage you to read this book with an open mind and a willingness to try something new.

Get ready to be amazed at how quickly you can take charge of your life now.

60-Second Reader

1. You get to choose which life experiences you'll have.
2. You have the power to create the life you want and deserve.
3. The power to create permanent positive change is available to you, no matter what you are struggling with.
4. You can learn to:
    - Challenge your old negative belief patterns
    - Stop unhealthy thoughts and feelings
    - Create positive life experiences for yourself
    - Stay calm and in control in any situation
    - Unleash the power of your mind to create the life you want and deserve
    - You can learn to be happy.

Self-Reflection

Take five minutes to think about how your life will be once you can stop those negative thoughts from occurring and instead, focus on the positives of every situation. What would that look like? What would you do? How would your life be different?

Use your imagination and have fun with this self-reflection. Write down all the wonderful things you'll finally be able to do. Remember to dream big!

_____

_____

_____

_____

_____

_____

_____

_____

_____

_____

_____

_____

_____

_____

_____

_____

_____

CHAPTER 2

Your Conscious vs. Your Subconscious Mind

To take control of your mind, it is important to understand the differences between the conscious and the subconscious mind and the roles that each part of your mind plays in your life.

Your Conscious Mind

The conscious part of your mind is your logical self. It can see the past, present, and future. It solves problems and stores your goals and dreams. It has free will to reject or accept concepts and ideas.

There are three main things to know and remember about your conscious mind:

1. It's responsible for logic, reasoning, and decision-making.

2. It controls all of your intentional actions.
3. It acts as a filtering system, rejecting or accepting information.

What Does This Mean?

The conscious part of your mind is the part that you are aware of. It's the part of your mind that you use when you are learning a new concept. For example, it helps you to learn how to ride a bike. When you are in the learning phase, you are consciously focused on how to balance yourself, how to pedal, how to move forward without crashing into something or losing your balance. All those thoughts and actions are the work of your conscious mind—something you are fully aware of.

Your conscious mind is also responsible for collecting data, processing the data, and making decisions based on the data at hand. It is the part of your mind that makes simple decisions such as, "I want to wear that black sweater because it looks good with my jeans." It also makes more complicated decisions, such as what college to apply to base on the career path you desire.

While your conscious mind is amazing in its ability to collect, process, and make sense of the data, it has its limitations. Did you know that your conscious mind can only process less than one percent of all the data available to you at any moment?

At any given time, you can only consciously focus on less than one percent of all the things that are going on within yourself and your environment.

Even if you could process ten times this amount, you would still be missing ninety percent of the facts and data available to you. That's an incomplete picture if you ask me.

Knowing that now should cause you to ask some questions about your life experiences so far: "What have I been missing? What information did I not even detect? How would my life be different if I have access to different information?"

Later, I will explain this concept and show you how to use this knowledge to take control of your thoughts and actions so you can take control of your life. Before we dive into that, let's talk about your subconscious mind and its functions.

Your Subconscious Mind

Your subconscious mind reacts based on instincts, habits, and learning from past experiences that are programmed into what I call "the Master Plan."

The Master Plan is a detailed set of instructions (like a movie script) that tells your subconscious mind what to do. Your subconscious mind does not have free will. Any ideas, thoughts, or feelings that get into the subconscious part of your mind stay there.

There are five main things to know and remember about your subconscious mind:

1. It is responsible for all of your involuntary actions (breathing, heartbeat, etc.).
2. It is one hundred percent automatic and follows scripts; it has no ideas and thoughts of its own.
3. It stores ALL of your memories, life experiences, learned information, and beliefs.
4. Its main function is to keep you alive and "safe."
5. Your subconscious mind processes information through pictures and images (or what is call an "Internal Representation," or "IR" for short).

REMEMBER: The subconscious mind is that part of your mind that is NOT within your awareness. It works quietly behind the scenes, tucked away in a dark corner, so no one will notice it or its activities.

Unlike the conscious part of your mind that can only process up to one percent of the available data, your subconscious mind can process one hundred percent of every bit of data it encounters, every second! That's right... your subconscious mind is one hundred percent aware of everything that's happening within you and around you, every single second of every single day.

The Master Plan

When you were born, you were born with a "pre-programmed" Master Plan, which is a detailed set of instructions and algorithms that tells your subconscious mind what to do. In your infancy and early years, that Master Plan includes only rudimentary, yet very important instructions that tell your subconscious mind what to do to keep you alive—such as breathing or regulating your heartbeat.

This Master Plan also has information handed down from your parents and ancestors in the form of genetics, such as your hair and eye color.

However, you were not born with the Master Plan for your belief system, core values, or the things you will learn in the future. Most of the information you'll need to create the majority of this Master Plan will be given to you during the first seven years of your life by those who interact with regularly, and through your own life experiences.

Your Master Plan is ever-changing, a constant work in progress. It is always adapting and evolving based upon your current situation and the aspirations you have for yourself.

Your conscious mind is responsible for adding to the Master Plan based on your life experiences. In a future chapter, we will discuss how your conscious mind programs the Master Plan. For right now, just know that there is a Master Plan from which your subconscious mind operates.

Your Subconscious Mind Simplified

To simplify the concept and help you understand the power of your mind, I want you to think of your subconscious mind as nothing more than a room full of movies—a movie library of your very own. In your movie library are hundreds of thousands (or even millions!) of movies starring you and your life experiences.

Within this movie library, there is a recording device and a Movie Operator. Your Movie Operator's job is to follow the Master Plan, which is a pre-programmed set of detailed instructions and algorithms provided by your conscious mind. In this way, your conscious mind is like the writer and director, and your subconscious mind is the actor or actress carrying out the directions within the scripts.

The recording device within your subconscious mind is always "on" and actively recording everything you are experiencing, every second of every day. Every one of your experiences EVER—whether it's a thought, a feeling, or an action—are recorded as a movie.

Using the instructions in your Master Plan, your Movie Operator labels, sorts, and stores your movies into your subconscious mind's library. That Master Plan also tells your Movie Operator when to store or remove a movie from your "favorite playlist" and when to play a movie back to you.

Besides recording, sorting, storing, and playing your movies, your Movie Operator has a bigger job. That job is to protect you and keep you safe from any real or perceived danger. Similar to the first job, your conscious mind has also created a Master Plan of what to do in every potential situation. That's an enormous job, but the only tools your subconscious mind has are the movies it has recorded of you and the instructions in the Master Plan.

Who's the Boss?

Given the information presented so far, who do you think is the boss—your conscious mind or your subconscious mind?

If you choose your conscious mind, you are correct!

Your conscious mind is always the boss. It's the part of your mind capable of processing and analyzing data. It's the part of your mind that has free will to make decisions and can accept and reject information. It's the part of your mind that filters information to come up with the Master Plan.

Your Reality Exists Only in Your Mind

Do you remember when I said your conscious mind can only process less than one percent and your subconscious mind can process one hundred percent of the data you encounter? What does that mean?

To put things into perspective, your subconscious mind receives millions of bits of data every single second. Millions of bits of data every single second! Stop and take that in for a moment. Every single second of your life, your subconscious mind is bombarded with millions of bits of data, which is equivalent to all the words in seven volumes of average-sized books. That's a lot of information to process every single second.

Imagine what it would be like for you if you were aware of millions of bits of data every single second of your life. How would you feel if you were forced to process seven volumes of books every single second? Your conscious mind is just not capable of processing that much data. You would go into severe sensory overload and would most likely explode or shut down. Luckily for you, all of that is happening in the background of your subconscious mind and is not within your awareness.

Of the millions of bits of data, the conscious part of your mind can only process 126 bits of data per second. To show what this looks like, let's look back at the example of the millions of bits of data as being equivalent to all the words within seven volumes of books. Of the seven books that your subconscious mind is processing, your conscious mind can only see one word. One word! That one word, whichever one word that might be, is the only one that makes it into your awareness and becomes your reality.

I want you to stop and think about what that means. Imagine reading seven books and understanding only one word, thus believing that one word is, in fact, the only subject of those books. Is there something you might be missing?

The important takeaway here is to realize that each of us is most likely focusing on a different word that becomes our respective realities.

REMEMBER: Your reality only exists in your mind and nowhere else. You might have a similar experience to that of another person, but when you break it down into tiny details, you will find significant variations.

Try this exercise out for fun. Close your eyes and turn to a random page in this book and point to a word. Now, open your eyes and look at that word. Does this one word represent everything this book is about?

I can guarantee that the answer is no. This book is much more than the one word you've randomly picked, but that shows how your conscious reality might be twisted by the powerful filtering system of your mind.

The Importance Center

How does your mind decide which one word out of the seven volumes of books to focus your attention on? Within your mind, you have a part called the Reticular Activating System. The Reticular Activating System is responsible for many functions. In this book, I will focus on its role in creating your reality. I like to refer to the Reticular Activating System as the "Importance Center," or "IC" for short.

Remember when I mentioned the Master Plan before? The Master Plan is kept here in the IC and tells your subconscious mind what information to send to your conscious mind.

All of your significant information is stored here— your belief systems, your values, your significant emotional experiences, and your significant learning situations.

REMEMBER: Your Importance Center is as unique as your fingerprint. No two people have the exact same Importance Center. That is why you can be at the same event as someone else and have a completely different experience.

From the millions of bits of data it receives, your subconscious mind filters them through the IC. If it matches the content within your IC, that information gets delivered to your conscious awareness. If it doesn't match the content within the IC, your subconscious mind will either delete it, generalize it, or distort it to make it "fit" in with your Master Plan.

Let's say your mom bought a brand-new car—a white Honda Accord. Soon after, you begin to see the same vehicle in the same color as your mom's car everywhere you go. Did a bunch of people suddenly buy the same car as your mom?

No. Most likely, those cars have been on the road all along, but it wasn't an important detail for you until your mom bought the car. Once your mom made that purchase, the details of the car entered your IC and instruct your subconscious mind to bring it into your awareness.

You might be hyper-aware of white Honda Accords for a while, but once the car becomes old news, you stop seeing them nearly as much. Does this mean that tons of people sold their car and they are off the road? No. All it means is that, at this moment in your life, the Honda Accord is no longer of significant importance, so it doesn't get delivered to your conscious mind at every sighting.

It's important to note that the IC has short-term and long-term parameters or instructions that it's following. Short-term parameters are things that might be important to you right now, for a brief time—similar to what's in style right now or the newness of a song. It could be a few days, a few weeks, or even months, but short-term parameters have an end date.

Long-term parameters stay with you for long periods of time. Often, they stay with you permanently unless you purposefully remove those parameters. Long-term parameters can be as simple as learned activities such as riding your bike or more complex, such as your belief systems.

The Personal Assistant
You Didn't Know You Have

How would you like to have a personal assistant who is there for you 24/7? How amazing would it be to have not only such an assistant but one who eagerly awaits your every command and obeys those commands without questioning you? That sounds amazing, right?

What if I told you that you actually do have that personal assistant already, but you have been giving your assistant bad commands? Commands that are getting you the results you are experiencing right now. Results that you may no longer want. Would you want to learn more about your assistant and, more importantly, learn how to command your assistant to create the results you want?

You might have guessed by now that your subconscious mind is your personal assistant. Your subconscious mind's job is to deliver to you whatever experience you are looking for in the easiest and quickest way possible.

What you might not know is that every thought you have and every feeling you feel is a command to your subconscious mind to give you more of the same.

That's right. Every thought you have and every feeling you feel is a command to your subconscious mind, "This is what I want. Give me more!"

If you said, "I'm so stressed," your subconscious mind heard that as a command: "I want to be stressed. Look for evidence to support why I should be stressed. Give me more reasons to feel stressed."

Once you give that command, your subconscious mind will immediately look for stressful details in your environment. Details that could stress you out get pushed to your IC and into your awareness. In addition, your subconscious mind will also look in your movie library to find your stressful movies to play in the background for you. You are the boss. When you ask for stress, your subconscious mind is happy to deliver it to you.

Does this sound familiar? How many times have you felt stressed out about something, then started having stressful thoughts about something else and soon, you were overwhelmed with stress and other negative feelings? This is because whatever you focus on grows bigger.

REMEMBER: Whatever you are focusing on, you are telling your subconscious mind to give you more of that thing. It's like feeding a monster food and watching it grow out-of-control right in front of your own eyes.

The good news is that the process works both ways. This means that when you focus on something positive, that positive thing will also grow. If you are stressed out, you can focus on being calm instead.

Choosing Calm

You have an assistant who will obey your every command, so use your assistant to your benefit. In stressful moments, you can say to yourself, "Even though I feel stressed, I choose to be calm."

Say, "I choose to be calm" several times to catch your assistant's attention. After saying that three times, start repeating, "I am calm. I am calm. I am calm," repeatedly. As you repeat, "I am calm," imagine yourself doing something that calms you down. It might be reading a book, laying out on the beach, or taking a nice, soothing bath.

With these steps, you are telling your assistant, "Even though I am stressed, I choose to be calm. Calm looks like this. Go get it for me. Give me more of this." It makes it simple for your subconscious mind to bring you to calmness.

Regardless of what negative emotion you experience, I recommend that you give your assistant the command to bring you calmness. Calmness is a wonderful place to be. Being calm is like a reset; it shuts down the old negative movies, so you have a blank screen. From a place of calmness, it is easier to look at the current situation for what it is and make decisions that best suit your needs.

REMEMBER: *Whether you focus on the negative or the positive aspects of any event, you have to spend energy on those thoughts. Why not focus your energy on positive, powerful thoughts that will create the results you're looking for?*

What Does Google Have to Do With Your Mind?

Here's another detail that is important to command your subconscious mind effectively. Your subconscious mind is like a Google search engine. Whatever you type into the search bar, when you press "enter," you'll get results that match that search request.

Just like the Google search engine, your subconscious mind cannot process negative commands. When you give your subconscious mind a negative command, it will ignore the negative part of it and focus on the remaining part of the command.

This is because of the Internal Representation (or IR) that I mentioned in the very beginning when we talked about the subconscious mind.

Remember when I said that your subconscious mind processes information by creating pictures and movies? When I say, "Think of spilling milk," what picture came to mind for you? That is how your subconscious mind understands those words.

If I say, "Don't spill the milk," what picture comes to mind? You can't form a picture of "Don't spill the milk." What might pop up instead is a picture of you holding onto a cup or glass carefully or something similar. That is not the same as "Don't spill the milk." Your subconscious mind, like the Google search engine, cannot process negatives. It cannot make an IR of a "don't" or a "not."

With Google, if you type into the search bar, "Don't find me blue shoes," and press "enter," Google will deliver you tons of things related to blue shoes. It completely ignores the "don't" part.

Try it out for yourself. Do a Google search using "don't" and see what results you'll get. Better yet, let's do a simple experiment right now. Ready? Here it is. My command to you is, "Don't think of an orange elephant."

What happened? The first thing you thought of was an orange elephant, wasn't it? When you realized you were thinking of an orange elephant, you might try to force yourself to think of the elephant in a different color or think of something else entirely different. That's interesting, isn't it?

You should have some "aha" moments right now. Think back over the past week or two and consider what commands you have been giving to your subconscious mind that are causing you to have some of your negative feelings and experiences.

Now that you are aware of how your subconscious mind interprets instructions, be very aware of the thoughts you're thinking and the feelings you are feeling. If the thoughts or feelings are negative, you can choose differently instead. This is where the "I choose to be calm" instruction comes in handy. That thought lets your assistant know you have chosen to be calm instead of upset or stressed, or whatever you may have been feeling.

REMEMBER: You are the boss, and your subconscious mind is your assistant. If you catch yourself giving your subconscious mind a negative thought or bad command, do something about it. Your assistant will carry out whatever command you provide unless you consciously revise it.

Let's say your mom is making dinner. She asked if you would rather have chicken or fish. You said fish but immediately changed your mind to chicken. When you realized this, chances are you corrected yourself and told your mom you wanted chicken. I doubt that you would just sit there and expect she would read your mind and prepare chicken instead.

You could do the same thing with your subconscious mind. Let's say you thought, "I'm too angry to focus now," and you catch yourself thinking that. Rather than just letting it go, you can say, "Whoops, I mean I'm willing to focus." Or you can say, "Erase or delete that," or similar phrases to tell your subconscious mind what you want to do with the misinformation. You can also say, "I'm in control of what I focus on."

The "I choose to be calm" command works fantastic here, too. Commands like these are very powerful because they tell your subconscious mind exactly what you want.

60-Second Reader

1. Your conscious mind is your logical mind that learns, thinks, and decides.
   a. You use this part of your mind to focus on details and become aware of things.
   b. You can only consciously focus on one percent of what's happening inside of you and around you at any given moment.
2. Your subconscious mind is like a program, running automatically in the background of your mind.
   a. You do not have an awareness of, nor can you focus on the automatic programs of your subconscious mind.
   b. Your subconscious mind can process one hundred percent of everything happening inside and immediately around you.
3. Your "Importance Center," or "IC," contains the automatic programs of your subconscious mind.
   a. Your beliefs and other significant information are stored in your IC.
   b. Your subconscious mind is programmed to look for evidence to support whatever is in your IC.
   c. Your IC is unique to you. No one else has the exact same IC as you, which also means no one else experiences things the way you do.

4. Your subconscious mind is your Personal Assistant and you are the Boss.
    a. It's programmed to give you the experiences you ask for in the easiest, quickest way possible.
    b. Problem: Every thought you have and feeling you feel is a command to your subconscious mind, "This is what I want; give me more!"
5. Your mind is like a Google search engine. It cannot process negative commands.
    a. When you give a negative command, such as "Don't be angry," your subconscious mind will ignore the "don't" and will carry out the rest of the command.

    Solution: Give your mind clear, positive commands of what you truly want. Instead of saying, "I don't want to be angry," you can say, "I choose to be calm."

Notes

Notes

_____

_____

_____

_____

_____

_____

_____

_____

_____

_____

_____

_____

_____

_____

_____

_____

_____

_____

_____

_____

_____

_____

_____

_____

_____

_____

_____

_____

CHAPTER 3

The Belief System

B elief:
   1. An acceptance that a statement is true, or that something exists
   2. Something one accepts as true or real; a firmly held opinion or conviction

Did you know that most of your belief systems were developed by the time you're seven years old? Did you also know that most of your belief systems were not decided by you but, in fact, were given to you by someone else?

I want you to stop and let that sink in for a bit. Most of your belief systems about who you are and the world around you were given to you from birth to the age of seven.

Why birth to seven years old? During this part of your growth and development, your subconscious mind is fully formed and operational. However, your conscious mind, the logical part of your mind, is just beginning to form and is not fully working yet. This is why little kids believe in everything they see or hear. The Easter Bunny, Santa Claus, and the Tooth Fairy are all one hundred percent real to your younger self because your conscious mind is not developed enough to say "No, that's not true."

The Creation of Beliefs

There are five main ways for you to develop a new belief:

1. Evidence: This is a rational decision based on cause and effect. For example, every time you break curfew, you get grounded. You will create a belief that breaking curfew results in being grounded.

2. Tradition: This is based on your family and cultural values. For example, you're raised in a Catholic family, your belief system will carry many facets of the Catholic teachings.

3. Authority: This is based on what the people in respected roles teach you or tell you about something. An example would be your doctor diagnosed you with depression; therefore, you believe you have depression.

4. Association: This is based on the people you interact with. For example, if you belong to the Mensa Club and interact with a bunch of

intellectuals, you might believe that intelligence is valued.

5. Revelation: This is based on your gut feelings, insights, and intuitions. For example, sometimes you just have that gut feeling of "I don't trust this person," although you might not know why.

Your subconscious mind records one hundred percent of everything, but that doesn't mean everything you experience becomes part of your belief system. In the beginning, when you do not have a Master Plan for new ideas or a belief system yet, your subconscious mind just records your events. It doesn't have a label for those events yet, nor is there a way for it to sort and categorize them.

Everything your subconscious mind records at this point is stored in a "general" category. In fact, in your mind's movie library are many categories of beliefs, similar to "genres" or "types" of movies. The four main movie types are:

1. Instructional: These are things you've learned to do such as riding a bike or playing the guitar.

2. Factual: These are things you've learned to accept as truth, like different colors or your date of birth.

3. Emotional: These are the experiences you've had and what the experiences mean to you specifically.

4. General: This is where all the miscellaneous movies are stored.

Let's look closely at how an instructional movie might get made. Imagine you are an eight-month-old infant learning how to use a spoon. If you have seen a baby learning how to use a spoon, you know how messy that process is. Often, the baby is shoveling food onto her chin or cheeks or drops it onto herself completely. That is because there is no instructional tape in her subconscious mind's library that tells her how to feed herself properly yet.

The first time you tried to feed yourself, your subconscious mind records the event and stores that movie in the general category of your movie library. The second time you attempted to feed yourself, your subconscious mind records it and stores it in the general category again. The third time you tried to feed yourself, your conscious mind might recognize the same data pattern and tell your subconscious mind to sort and store them together.

Once you fully know how to use a spoon to feed yourself, it becomes an instructional video for "Feeding Self with a Spoon." The next time you go to feed yourself, your subconscious mind replays that movie in the background, and you feed yourself easily without thinking about it.

Consciously, a lot of things were happening simultaneously for your subconscious mind to sort and categorize that movie. Perhaps your mom said, "Let's learn how to use a spoon today" or something similar every time she handed you a spoon. With repetition, you consciously learn that when your mom says, "Let's learn how to use a spoon today," and hands you an object; that object is called a spoon, and it is used to put food in your mouth. You then use this information to create your instructional video.

Major belief systems are created similarly, either through a single significant emotional event or repetitions of several low-intensity emotional events.

Significant Emotional Events

Imagine that you are three years old and you're playing in your room. Like most three-year-olds, you are making a huge mess, throwing things around, and having a great time. Your mom comes into the room, sees the mess, and gets furious with you. She might force you to quit playing and clean your room. She might yell at you or, if you're in an abusive situation, you might get hit on the head or kicked or something similar.

This is definitely a significant emotional event for your three-year-old self. You were just having fun in your room when suddenly your mom grabbed your toys away, hit you on the back of your head, and yelled, "You're a bad girl. Clean up your room now!" You don't have a full understanding of what just happened. All you know is that your fun ended, your mom is angry, and you are in pain. Because this event was so traumatic and the pain was significant, your conscious mind immediately accepts this to be a fact and creates one or more beliefs about this event.

Some beliefs that might develop from this incident are:

1. Having fun is bad. When I have fun, I get punished.

2. I am a bad girl. I made Mom angry.
3. I am helpless. There is nothing I can do to fix this.
4. I am not loved.

These and other potential beliefs become a part of your Master Plan with instructions and strategies on how to avoid these painful events.

Your subconscious mind recorded the whole event, labeled it, and filed it under all the applicable beliefs. Because there are instructions in the Master Plan about this event, this movie gets placed into the IC immediately. Your subconscious mind is now programmed to look for evidence of these beliefs and to bring matching details to your conscious awareness immediately.

Repetitive Low-Intensity Emotional Events

Imagine again that you are a three-year-old, playing in your room and making a huge mess. Your mom came into the room, saw the mess, and said in a soft but stern voice, "Look at this mess. You're a bad girl." Your mom might take your toy away, or she might make you clean it up. You were having fun, and she interrupted it.

The emotions attached to this event are low in intensity. You might be upset, but it wasn't a significant emotional event. Still, your subconscious mind recorded it and filed this movie away in the general category of your movie library.

If this happened repeatedly, it becomes a different story. Let's say the exact scenario happened again three days later. Your subconscious mind makes the same recording and filed it away with the first recording. At this point, these videos are not important yet. However, let's say it happened again two to three more times. Your conscious mind might create these beliefs:

1. Having fun is bad. When I have fun, I get punished.
2. I am a bad girl. I make Mom unhappy.
3. I am helpless. I want to play, but Mom won't let me.

Similar to the significant emotional event example, if this happened repeatedly, your conscious mind would include this data in the Master Plan, thus telling your subconscious mind to look for evidence to support these belief systems.

Remember, beliefs are created whenever you have a significant emotional event or if something keeps happening repeatedly.

Here, Take This Belief and Make It Yours

Earlier, I said that most of your beliefs were given to you. How is that possible and why is that the case?

From birth to seven years old, your conscious mind is not fully formed or fully functional yet. If you hear something repeatedly, especially if it's from someone you love or who has authority over you, you will believe what they say is the truth.

For example, if you grew up in a poor household and heard your parents fight about money constantly or heard them say things like, "It is so hard to make money," or "Those greedy rich people," you might create a belief system of:

1. Money causes people to fight.
2. It's hard to make money.
3. Rich people are greedy.

Similarly, if you grew up with a man-hating angry mother who constantly said, "You can't trust men," "All men are pigs," or "All men are controlling," you would also believe these generalities to be true about men.

Remember, low-intensity repetitive events and significant emotional events create beliefs.

Sleuthing for Evidence

Let's pretend that the incident with the three-year-old I mentioned above happened to you and now, you have a belief of "I am a bad person." Once a recording is placed into the IC, your mind is being directed to look for evidence to support that belief system for the rest of your life.

You carry your belief system with you wherever you go. It's like carrying a basket around with you for the rest of your life to look for evidence to put into it. If a friend, uncle, or aunt says, "You're a bad person," you'll pick this information up and put it into your basket to validate your belief system. Same with any comments from anyone else that matches the belief system.

Soon enough, you are carrying a basket full of evidence to support why you are such a bad person. It feels heavy, burdensome, and overwhelming to have to carry this extra weight everywhere you go. You become tired and you have no energy or motivation to do the things you want to.

Because you have a belief system of "I'm a bad person" in your IC, your subconscious mind will only shift data that matches that belief system into your awareness. If someone said, "You are such an amazing person," you either don't hear them at all, or you hear them, but don't believe it. In fact, you might even try to prove that the other person is wrong.

A good example of this is to think of a time when someone has given you a simple compliment that made you feel uncomfortable. How did you respond? You might have said nothing because you didn't know how to react since you don't believe what they've said. You might have deflected that compliment, given credit to someone else, or downplayed it completely because you were uncomfortable. You may even interpret their words as sarcasm or false flattery.

Changing Beliefs

Although most of your belief systems were developed between birth to seven years old, you can create new belief systems after seven.

Any time you experience a significant emotional event once or a low-intensity emotional event repeatedly, you can create new belief systems. You can also develop new belief systems when you, on purpose, decide you want to change.

Some beliefs are easy to change because they are in your awareness. When your belief is within your awareness, you can decide what you want to do with it. Deeply buried beliefs are much harder to change. Even then, changing your subconscious belief system is definitely possible. It requires working with someone knowledgeable on how to help you access the contents of your subconscious mind and deliver them to your conscious awareness in a safe and gentle way.

60-Second Reader

a. Most of your belief systems were developed from birth to seven years old.

    a. Your conscious mind, the logical part of your mind, is just beginning to form and is not fully working until around the time you turn seven.

    b. This is why little kids believe everything they see or hear.

b. Beliefs are created whenever:

    a. You have a significant emotional event.

    b. Something happens frequently.

c. Once you create a belief, it goes into your IC and your subconscious mind is programmed to look for evidence to support it.

d. Although most of your belief systems were developed between birth and seven years old, you can create new belief systems after seven.

    a. Any time you experience a significant emotional event once or a low-intensity emotional event repeatedly, you can create new belief systems.

    b. You can also develop new beliefs when you, on purpose, decide you want to change.

Notes

Notes

_____

_____

_____

_____

_____

_____

_____

_____

_____

_____

_____

_____

_____

_____

_____

_____

_____

_____

_____

_____

_____

_____

_____

_____

CHAPTER 4

The Stranger Danger Protocol

How many times have you been told that in order for you to accomplish something, all you have to do is use your willpower? And how many times have you tried using your willpower, and yet, you did not achieve your goals?

You might have been frustrated or disappointed with yourself. You might even become angry with yourself. You might even believe that you are a failure.

It is very common for people to start a goal with excitement and determination, then give up on it soon after. This is because their conscious desires do not match the subconscious beliefs they have programmed into their Master Plan.

*Willpower doesn't work if your
subconscious belief systems do not align
with your goal.*

Let's use a common scenario to illustrate this. Pretend you want to lose ten pounds. You read a news article that inspired you. It says if you eat under thirteen hundred calories daily and exercise three times per week for thirty minutes each time, you'll lose ten pounds in two weeks.

You think, "Wow! All I have to do is keep my caloric intake to less than thirteen hundred calories per day and exercise thirty minutes a day, three times a week; I'll lose ten pounds in two weeks! It seems simple enough, plus it's only two weeks! I can do this!" You set on your weight loss path with determination and even perhaps some excitement.

Soon after you started this new healthy program, something changed that inevitably stops you from moving forward in achieving your goals. That something is your subconscious mind, and it screams, "Change is scary; change is dangerous."

Remember earlier, I said your subconscious mind's primary aim is to keep you safe? Well, safe doesn't mean "safe" according to your subconscious mind.

Your subconscious mind is programmed to accept that "safe" means "DO NOT CHANGE. CHANGE IS SCARY. CHANGE IS DANGEROUS! STAY EXACTLY AS YOU ARE RIGHT NOW!"

Whenever you attempt to make a change that disrupts the status quo of your current belief system, your subconscious mind freaks out. It assumes that you are in danger and it will do everything it can to get you back to its perceived safety.

Let's look at the weight loss example again. For the sake of this example, pretend you are three hundred pounds and everyone in your family weighs three hundred pounds. Also imagine you have been struggling to lose weight all your life.

Imagine reading an article that motivates and inspires you to take actions to lose weight again. You're excited! This is the thing that will finally help you lose weight! This is your answer!

When you decided to follow the new program, that was a conscious decision. As you do the prescribed activities, you feel good about yourself. You feel hopeful because you are still within the safety zone according to your subconscious mind. As you move away from the safety zone and into a new territory, or "the danger zone," your subconscious mind freaks out and thinks you're in danger. Since its job is to keep you safe, it will do all that it can to get you back to its perceived safety zone. It activates the "Stranger Danger Protocol."

> **REMEMBER:** *The purpose of the Stranger Danger Protocol is to make you doubt yourself, put you in a place of fear, or make you feel bad by reliving past failures, so YOU STOP what you're doing and go back to where it feels safe.*

To get you to stop your new activities, your subconscious mind might play your old movies that cause you to doubt yourself. Movies that make you think, "Can I do this?"

"What would make me think this would even work?"

"I've tried so many things, and nothing worked!"

"It's genetic and there's nothing I can do about it."

Or it might play fearful movies. "It will be so hard to exercise three times a week. It will aggravate my left knee again!" Or perhaps, "It will be so boring eating nothing but fish and vegetables. I can't even be social; everyone I know only eats burgers and fries!"

Perhaps your subconscious mind might play movies of your past failures. Maybe you've lost five pounds in the past only to gain ten pounds back. It will replay those old movies, causing you to re-experience the old pain of failure.

Not only are the old painful movies playing in the background, but your subconscious mind will actively scan your environment looking for evidence to show you why you will fail.

If you are like most people, when you have doubts, fears, or you remember your past failures, you will stop doing those new activities and go back to your old ways. It seems too scary or even pointless to try.

Every time you start and stop like this, you strengthen your "I can't" belief system. Soon, the belief system becomes so heavy and so powerful that all you have to do is think about your goal and you'll go into an anxious state.

The Root of Most Problems

The Stranger Danger Protocol is not the only tool your subconscious mind has to keep you from changing. In your subconscious mind's library catalog are the four main themes I've mentioned, Instructional, Factual, Emotional, and General.

Within the Emotional Category are four main subcategories:

1. I'm Not Good Enough.
2. I'm Not Worthy.
3. I'm Not Loved.
4. I'm Not Safe.

We all have these four main subcategories in our IC. It is part of our Master Plan, created by us, to keep ourselves safe. It is also the root of most problems that we, as humans, encounter. How many movies you have in each of these subcategories depends on you, your beliefs, and your life experiences.

The details of your movies differ from other people because your movies are based on your specific life experiences and belief systems. However, regardless of who you are, these four main subcategories are there in varying degrees, hidden in a dark corner, ready to unleash at any moment.

In the next few chapters, I will discuss each of these belief systems further. But right now, let's imagine one of your big belief systems or emotional subcategories is, "I'm Not Good Enough." Because this is a significant belief system, it is housed in your IC and your subconscious mind is programmed to constantly look for evidence to support this. No matter where you are, no matter what you are doing, no matter who you're with, your subconscious mind is constantly looking for evidence to support that you're not good enough.

Imagine in the background of your mind is a movie playing on a repetitive loop, 24/7, of all the instances that prove you're not good enough. This movie plays on and on, getting louder and louder as you attempt to do anything that might threaten or contradict this belief system.

Imagine that 24/7, you are receiving messages of "You're not good enough." These constant negative thoughts and feelings keep you stuck. The fear and doubts that often go hand-in-hand with these messages prevent you from taking actions and moving forward because it seems too scary or pointless to fight a losing battle.

Most of the time, you are unaware of the movies your subconscious mind is playing in the background for you. However, as you continue to challenge any significant belief system, the applicable movies get louder and more vivid; you might even get a conscious awareness of bits of it. However, most of the time, you are not fully aware of the exact cause of your underlying belief system. You might have a feeling of fear, anxiety, or discomfort that you can't fully explain.

Taming Your Subconscious Mind

What do you do when you want to change an underlying belief? How can you change your behaviors and belief systems when your subconscious mind is fighting you every step of the way?

The first step is to recognize that you are the boss and your subconscious mind is only following the instructions you have programmed into your Master Plan. Because you are the boss and you are the one responsible for programming the Master Plan, you can also change the Master Plan.

To begin, you want to acknowledge your negative emotions and decide you want to make a change. Next, create small, simple goals for yourself. In the case of the ten-pound weight loss, your small, simple goal might be to lose just one pound. Then, perhaps step it up to three pounds, then five pounds, eight pounds, and finally, ten pounds.

When you first start on this journey, you'll feel good because you're doing what you consciously wanted to do, and you are within your safety zone. Soon after, you will enter the perceived danger zone and your subconscious mind will start freaking out. It will reach for and play your old, negative movies again.

However, this time, your goal is small and simple. You push through the slight discomfort to reach your first small and simple goal. Once you reach your first goal, your subconscious mind cannot deny that you have met the goal. To keep your subconscious mind stable, you do whatever you need to do to maintain the one-pound weight loss.

Do not attempt to lose any more weight at this point. You hang out at your new weight for a while to allow your subconscious mind to realize that you are "safe" and that this is your new normal. From that new starting point, you push again until you reach the next goal. As before, when you reach your next goal, you just hang out there for a little while to allow your subconscious mind to establish this as a new safety zone.

How long you have to hang out depends on the belief system you are challenging, how long that belief system has been around, and the emotional charges attached to it. You will know it is time to work on the next small, simple goal when you feel comfortable and it is effortless to maintain your current achievement.

You might be wondering, "If my conscious mind is the boss, why can't I just change the Master Plan at will? Why do I need to make these small, simple goals?"

Your conscious mind is, in fact, the boss and you can, in fact, change the parameters within the Master Plan. You can change the details within your Master Plan easily when the belief is within your awareness and is of low emotional intensity.

However, when you experience something with significant negative emotions, you learn that it is too painful, and you don't want to experience that emotion again. To make sure you never experience that pain again, when you program your Master Plan around that experience, you put up as many booby traps as you can to protect the Master Plan. This is why you have to take small, simple steps to diffuse the booby traps without setting off the alarm.

If you take these small, simple steps in real life, it might take years to accomplish your goals depending on what they are. I know you don't want to wait years to achieve your goals. You want to achieve your goals now, or at least in a relatively short amount of time.

The cool thing is that there are simpler, more effective ways to achieve these goals quickly. For one, you can speed up the process significantly by vividly seeing yourself completing your goals and completing them well repeatedly. This works because your subconscious mind is constantly creating movies for you.

The good news is that your subconscious mind can't tell the difference between a real event you're experiencing versus something you are vividly imagining. To your subconscious mind, it is the same. It records, sorts, and stores them both the same way.

You can use this information to your advantage. Let's say you have a goal to be comfortable and confident in doing a class presentation. Vividly see yourself standing up in front of the classroom, feeling good about yourself and feeling confident that you know your material well. Vividly see yourself presenting with a strong and assured voice, making great eye contact and feeling at ease. Vividly imagine yourself completing the presentation and answering questions with authority and confidence.

As you imagine these scenarios, bring in as much detail as you can. Use all of your senses. See it. Touch it. Hear it. Taste it. Smell it. Feel the emotions attached to it. The more details that you provide, the better your recording will be and the quicker the change will occur.

Sports stars have been using this technique for centuries with amazing results! A tennis star, for example, might vividly imagine himself performing a perfect serve repeatedly—perhaps twenty times before a match. When he steps onto the court for his first serve, his mind thinks it is the twenty-first serve. His mind is calm and focused. His body is relaxed. He carries out his serve with confidence and power. This simple little technique can help you achieve any goal in your life easier and quicker.

While this technique is very useful in helping you achieve many of your goals, other goals are harder to achieve with this method alone, especially if they are deeply rooted in your belief systems. For example, if your father regularly beats you from the time you were an infant to the time he left when you were nine years old, it might seem almost impossible to forgive him. You can definitely use the visualization technique mentioned above and achieve your goals, but that could take significant effort and dedication because of all the booby traps you have laid around this belief system.

In instances of deep-rooted, especially traumatic beliefs, it is best to involve the guidance of a highly trained professional who specializes in addressing the subconscious mind. They can help you identify your troubling belief system, the source of its creation, and the negative emotions attached to them.

Once the negative emotions are identified and released, the belief becomes neutralized; you are then free to reprogram that part of the Master Plan.

REMEMBER: When your conscious and subconscious minds are in conflict, your subconscious mind always wins.

To be successful in creating your desired changes, you must resolve your issues at the root of the problem—that means addressing your subconscious mind. Failing to do so will cause you to revisit that problem repeatedly. The most effective therapies for changing deep-rooted belief systems address the subconscious mind directly.

In the coming chapters, I will share stories of some real-life clients of mine who resolved their problems quickly once they understood how to address their subconscious mind. I will share their main emotional subcategory and how it showed up in their lives. See if you can relate with one or more of them to begin your own self-discovery.

60-Second Reader

1. Willpower doesn't work if the goal you want to achieve is not aligned with your subconscious belief systems.

2. Your subconscious mind's primary aim is to keep you safe.

    a. Safe doesn't mean "safe" according to your subconscious mind.

    b. To your subconscious mind, change is scary. Change is dangerous.

    c. Whenever you attempt to change something that disrupts your current belief system, your subconscious mind freaks out. It thinks you're in danger and it will do everything it can to get you back to your "safe" place.

3. Your subconscious mind uses the Stranger Danger Protocol to get you back to your "safe" spot.

    a. The Stranger Danger Protocol will make you doubt yourself, make you fearful, or make you feel bad by reliving past failures, so YOU STOP what you're doing and go back to where it feels "safe" again.

4. Most problems can be traced back to one or more of four faulty beliefs:

    a. I'm not enough.

    b. I'm not worthy.

  c. I'm not loved.

  d. I'm not safe.

5. To tame your subconscious mind, start by being the Boss of your mind. Give your subconscious mind clear and direct commands.

  a. Create small, simple goals that lead to the ultimate big goal to prevent the Stranger Danger Protocol from being activated.

6. Your subconscious mind does not know the difference between what's real and what's imagined. To your subconscious mind, it's the same.

  a. Whatever you want to achieve, vividly imagine yourself already achieving that goal. Be sure to attach strong, positive emotions as you imagine your achievements to help your subconscious mind quickly accept it as "safe."

  b. This simple little technique can help you achieve any goal in your life easier and quicker.

7. When your conscious and subconscious minds are in conflict, your subconscious mind always wins.

Notes

Notes

_____

_____

_____

_____

_____

_____

_____

_____

_____

_____

_____

_____

_____

_____

_____

_____

_____

_____

_____

_____

_____

_____

_____

CHAPTER 5

I'm Not Good Enough

I'm not good enough is the biggest, darkest emotional subcategory in your movie library. At the root of most problems is an underlying belief that you're not good enough.

Before you dismiss this notion as a possibility, know this belief is often hidden under the surface of your conscious thinking and can still be a significant source of trouble for you.

This belief system might show up as:

- I'm not [insert your word here] enough (i.e., smart, tall, beautiful, funny, old).
- I can't seem to do anything right.
- Others are always doing better than I am.
- I have nothing important to contribute.
- There is something wrong with me.
- I'm not good at anything.

Case Study: Stressed-Out Samantha
Client: Samantha, Age 15½

Presenting Problem

Samantha had been becoming more withdrawn over the past few months. Her mother is concerned because she suddenly lost 20 pounds, has no appetite, and is having difficulty keeping up in school. Samantha used to be a straight "A" student, but now she is struggling to keep passing grades. Currently, she is at-risk for failing one class because she is behind on several writing assignments. She is also getting a "C" in another class.

Samantha reports feeling overwhelmed by the ever-increasing stress and responsibilities. She has a difficult time saying "no" and, as a result, she does whatever people ask of her. She takes on too many tasks and then feels burdened by the commitments. As a result of feeling overwhelmed, Samantha has a difficult time focusing during the day and sleeping at night. Simple tasks are now difficult.

Family History

Samantha's parents were divorced when she was eight years old. She currently lives with her mom and two younger brothers. She describes the relationship between her mom, siblings, and herself as being pretty good. For a while, she was seeing her dad every month since the divorce. That relationship is described as extremely stressful because "I could never make him happy." In fact, it's so stressful that she hasn't seen or spoken to her father for close to a year. He rarely attempts to contact her.

Social History

Samantha is shy and has a few close friends. She used to enjoy hanging out with them, but lately, she finds it hard to enjoy herself socially. Samantha reports having difficulty opening up to people, even to her close friends.

Words Samantha Often Heard Others Used to Describe Her

Smart, studious, giving, nice, mature, responsible, generous

Words Samantha Uses to Describe Herself

People pleaser, weak, can't say "no," invisible, and pushover

Session One Notes

Growing up with her father was difficult for Samantha. Her parents fought constantly. There were many screaming and yelling bouts between her parents. Whenever her parents would fight, her father would belittle Samantha. He would be demanding, verbally abusive, and always had to be right. He was cold and distant.

Samantha can't recall her father ever saying, "I love you," or "I'm proud of you." When she tried to hug him, she was mostly pushed aside or told to go play somewhere else.

From a very early age, Samantha tried everything she could think of to get her father to like her. She would play quietly when he was around. She tried to do her best in school and even played sports that she didn't care for, just because her father liked the sport. Occasionally, her effort would pay off and her dad would give her some attention.

While Samantha was not completely aware, the theme for Samantha going through life was, "I'm not good enough."

Root Cause

We traced back to an incident when Samantha was five years old. After a horrendous fight between her parents, Samantha decided to draw a picture for her father to cheer him up. Samantha spent a long time perfecting it; drawing and erasing, redrawing and erasing until she thought it was perfect. When she was finally satisfied with her work, she excitedly approached her father. With a big smile on her face, Samantha presented her artwork and said, "I drew this picture for you, Daddy. I hope this makes you happy."

Her father looked over at her briefly and didn't say a word or make any attempt to reach out to receive his gift. Samantha stood silently and held her breath for what seemed like hours to her. Still, there was no response from her father. Slowly, Samantha approached him with his gift stretched out in front of her. Her father grabbed it, looked at it, and said, "You think this is going to make everything better? Look at it. It's so sloppy. There's nothing good about this picture!" He then crumpled up the drawing, threw it in the corner, and went back to ignoring Samantha.

Samantha stood there motionless, too scared to cry or move.

In that very moment, Samantha recalls feeling:

1. Angry: How can he be so mean? Even if he didn't like it, he doesn't have to treat me that way.
2. Confused: Why didn't he like it? I spent so much time and energy on it. I thought it was pretty and that it would make him happy.
3. Self-doubt: Do I even know what pretty is? Am I sloppy? I can't seem to do anything right. What's wrong with me?
4. Fear: His anger is always so scary to me. He is so cold. I can never tell what he will do next.
5. Sad: My father doesn't love me. I'm unlovable.
6. Helpless: I can't change the situation. There's nothing I can do.
7. Self-hate: I'm no good. I can't do anything right. I can't make my dad happy.

As Samantha recalled the story, she felt significant anger toward her father. She couldn't understand how someone could be so cruel. Samantha now recognized how this single significant emotional event resulted in her pattern of trying to please everyone as an attempt to feel valued and loved.

After working on releasing the anger, Samantha revisited the memory with a new perspective. She recognized that her father was unhealthy, and his actions reflected the way he felt about himself. Samantha finally understood it was not about her at all. She was just a convenient and easy target for his anger. She decided to forgive her dad.

Samantha could not believe how much of a burden it was to seek her father's approval continuously. She felt liberated and excited to learn to be the source of her own "approval machine," as she called it.

Three-Month Follow-Up

Samantha has reconnected with her father. She finally told him how much his actions had hurt her. She also told him she forgave him. Samantha reports being very surprised when her father became teary and hugged her. Her father even apologized and promised to do better. It was a wonderful day for Samantha.

Samantha also reported:

1. She is all caught up in her classes and is passing all of them.
2. She feels good about herself.
3. She sleeps better now and is more focused when she is at school.
4. She is more aware of her own needs and can say "no" to activities that do not interest or suit her.
5. She feels more confident in who she is and what she is capable of.

Six-Month Follow-Up

Samantha's relationship with her father is still distant. He did make some minor efforts to tell her he is happy with her occasionally. However, he still acts cold and is often aloof. Samantha now realizes that her father is not mentally healthy and no longer takes his actions as a personal attack or a reflection of who she is.

Samantha reports that she is going out with her friends so much more. She feels comfortable and at ease when she is out. Something that surprised her is that she feels much more adventurous than she ever thought she would.

Lesson Learned

Samantha had always wanted to please people. She did not understand why she felt that way. Even when she was overwhelmed, she still couldn't say "no." This was because of that significant emotional event she had experienced at age five that caused her to believe she wasn't good enough for her dad. She felt unlovable, so she continued to do everything she could to earn his love.

Occasionally, her efforts paid off and her father gave her the attention she had been craving. This reinforced to Samantha that to be loved, she must do everything she could to prove that she is good enough and worthy of love.

Once she neutralized the emotions attached to this incident, she could see the situation for what it was and realized the error of this belief system. The problem wasn't that she was not good enough; the problem was that her father was not emotionally healthy enough to show Samantha love in a warm or consistent manner.

Realizing this allowed Samantha to consciously change her beliefs and recognize her true self-worth. She no longer needs validation from others to feel good about herself.

REMEMBER: There are always more sides to the story than just your side and things are most often not what they seem at first.

When things are not going well for you, rather than focusing on what's wrong and making the problem bigger, ask yourself, "How else can I see this situation differently?" Have fun with this question. Be a detective and look for clues that point to the possibilities of different conclusions, happier conclusions.

When you have a strong negative reaction to something, you can bet that there is an underlying belief at play. Be willing to pause, examine the situation, and identify the potential negative beliefs, or "trigger," for your feelings. Be willing to let go of your original thought or belief and become open to seeing evidence of the new (and improved) conclusions you've just created. You might just find yourself pleasantly surprised.

Self-Reflection

What is your biggest take-away from this chapter?

_____

_____

_____

_____

_____

_____

_____

_____

_____

_____

_____

_____

_____

_____

_____

_____

_____

_____

_____

How can you use what you've just learned to take charge of your mind and be a happier, more confident you?

_____

_____

_____

_____

_____

_____

_____

_____

_____

_____

_____

_____

_____

_____

_____

_____

_____

_____

_____

_____

_____

_____

_____

_____

CHAPTER 6

I'm Not Worthy

Many times, the "I'm not good enough" and "I'm not worthy" beliefs go hand-in-hand. It often looks like this, "I don't deserve _____ because I'm not _____."

This belief system might show up as:
• I don't deserve to be successful because I'm lazy.
• I don't deserve this award because I'm not smart.

"I'm not worthy" can also result from having guilty feelings because of something you have done in the past.

Case Study: Miserable Megan
Client: Megan, Age 18

Presenting Problem

Megan sought help because she was recently diagnosed with depression and was prescribed Zoloft and weekly counseling. Megan attended nine sessions and stopped going because she did not notice any improvement. She also stopped taking her Zoloft due to dizziness, headaches, and stomach pain while she was on it.

Megan reported being "cursed with uncontrollable negative thoughts." No matter what was happening, Megan would play out negative scenarios in her mind. She feels consumed with these negative feelings and thinks she's losing control of her mind. Even when things are going well, Megan reports feeling anxious and fearful that "something bad" was about to happen.

The situation was so bad that Megan had to quit her part-time job at the local movie theater because she was too emotional and cried easily.

Family History

Megan is an only child and reports having had a better-than-average childhood. Her parents were and still are loving and supportive. Her mom and dad often praise her and brag about her to others constantly. Megan recalls hearing her parents say things like, "Megan is so perfect. We are so lucky to have such a wonderful daughter," and "I wouldn't know what to do if we had a problem child," referring to the girl next door.

Social History

Megan reports making friends easily. She has always been one of the popular girls in her school. She volunteers weekly at various local community centers.

Words Megan Often Heard Others Used to Describe Her

Beautiful, smart, funny, giving, generous, friendly, kind

Words Megan Uses to Describe Herself

Fake, phony, a bad person, ugly, unworthy, liar

Session One Notes

Megan was very closed off at first. She hardly made eye contact, preferring to hide her face behind the office pillows. Megan insisted she doesn't know why she feels she is a bad person, but just knows that she is. She consistently said, "I don't deserve to be happy. I've done many bad things and I can't change them." Megan would not discuss what those bad things were, but would say, "The people at work don't like me," and "I hurt people."

Session Three Notes

Megan is more comfortable and is opening up significantly—although cautiously—in each subsequent session. She shared several incidences that "prove" she's a bad person in her own eyes. She also shared a story of something that happened when she was twelve years old—the reason she hates herself so much and believes she is undeserving.

That year, Megan had entered middle school and started attending a new school. Although there were many new students, Megan felt very comfortable in her new environment and, as always, made friends easily. Like previous years, Megan began hanging out with the popular older girls within a few weeks. Life was easy for Megan.

For Megan's friend, Ashley, life was just getting difficult. Ashley had always been small, young looking for her age, and socially awkward. Being around the older girls made it even more obvious just how small and awkward she was. Ashley did not fit in and was an easy target at school.

Megan sobbed loudly as she recalled an incident when some popular girls started teasing Ashley about her awkwardness and size. Ashley began crying and looked over to Megan. "She was begging me to help her with her eyes," Megan cried.

For some unknown reason, Megan felt angry with Ashley for putting her in the middle of this situation. Unsure of what to do, Megan looked away and pretended not to notice the pain and humiliation Ashley had to endure. Although her inner voice said, "Do something!" Megan continued to pretend to be oblivious to Ashley's plight.

Megan cannot recall what happened after that but stated she felt so guilty for what had happened. She has not forgiven herself for being a coward. In fact, Megan admitted that all of her good deeds are just her effort to hide the fact that she was such an ugly and weak person.

Megan was hesitant to forgive herself at first. She was scared that if she let go of the guilt and shame, she would start engaging in those horrible activities again. After reassurance, Megan was willing to start the self-forgiveness process. At the end of that session, Megan reported feeling much better about who she was and what she had done.

Root Cause

Feeling lighter and more hopeful, Megan started working on discovering and eliminating other significant negative emotional events.

Megan was very shocked when a memory of an incident came up from when she was seven years old. Megan and her parents were over visiting at their neighbor's house for dinner one night. Megan and Riley (the neighbor's nine-year-old daughter) were playing in Riley's bedroom while the parents were in the kitchen, preparing dinner.

Megan spotted a pretty pink box and asked Riley to show her what was in it. Riley excitedly pulled out a new necklace her mother had just given her a week before and showed it to Megan with pride. Carefully, Riley put the necklace back into its box before returning to play with Megan.

After dinner, Riley's mother asked Riley to retrieve her new necklace to show Megan and her parents. Riley ran to her room and came back empty-handed.

Riley said the necklace was missing and accused Megan of stealing it. As soon as the accusation left Riley's mouth, her mother yanked her over and started shouting at her. "You lost your new necklace? You are so careless. You don't deserve anything nice. How can you blame little Megan for your carelessness? I'm so disappointed in you!"

Riley tried to defend herself, but her father stepped in and sternly told her to go to her room and "Think about the trouble you are causing for your mother."

Crying quietly, Riley left the room. On her way out, Riley looked at Megan, but Megan avoided her eyes, too ashamed of herself because she knew the truth.

Later that night, Megan went outside to throw the necklace away. Upon entering her house, Megan overheard her mother saying, "I can't believe that Riley. She is such a bad girl, blaming our little Megan like that. Megan is so perfect. I don't know what I would do with a problem child like that."

Megan felt sick to her stomach. She was certain that if her parents knew the truth, they wouldn't love her anymore. That night, Megan cried herself to sleep.

This memory surprised Megan as she hasn't thought about this incident for many years. Recalling it now, Megan felt so much shame and guilt again. She can't believe that she never confessed. In fact, over the next few weeks after that event, Riley had begged her to return the necklace several times. Each time, Megan would look away and say, "I don't know what you're talking about. You're a liar!"

With significant reassurance, Megan was willing to forgive herself and accept that she was just a little girl then, doing the best she knew how at the time, and it is now time to forgive herself and move on.

After several rounds of forgiveness work, Megan reported feeling significant relief. For the first time in many years, Megan finally saw herself as a good and kind person. She recognized that her kind acts were not an act. She truly enjoyed helping people. Megan could finally see herself for the kind and giving young woman she is.

Three-Month Follow-Up

Megan reports feeling happy and free. Megan credited her new outlook on life to her ability to forgive herself. Occasionally, the self-doubts would come back. Each time they came back, Megan overcame them by reaffirming, "I forgive myself. I am a good person. I am worthy of happiness."

Lesson Learned

Guilt is a powerful negative emotion that can hold us back and cause significant pain. In Megan's case, although she had forgotten about the incident with Riley, that incident was a significant emotional event for her that created a lot of negative beliefs.

Once she created the belief that she was a bad person—and therefore, did not deserve to be loved—she unknowingly programmed her mind to look for evidence to support that belief system. Her mind did exactly what she instructed it to do and made her hyper-aware of many incidences that matched this belief system. Many of those incidences were minor, yet still played an important part in validating her beliefs.

Forgiveness is the antidote to guilt. When you forgive yourself, you release the burden of guilt. That doesn't mean that you condone what you did, nor that you think it's okay to repeat the action. When you forgive yourself, you recognize and accept that you did the best that you knew how to do at the time. You give yourself permission to let go of the guilt so you can move forward in peace. From a place of peace, you can make much better decisions for yourself and your future.

REMEMBER: If you are holding guilty feelings about something, now is the right time to let it go. Give yourself permission to release it and forgive yourself. You do not need the guilt to avoid the same mistake or to "learn your lesson." Once you have forgiven yourself, you will become much freer and your decisions will be clearer.

Self-Reflection

What is your biggest take-away from this chapter?

_____

_____

_____

_____

_____

_____

_____

_____

_____

_____

_____

_____

_____

_____

_____

_____

_____

_____

_____

How can you use what you've just learned to take charge of your mind and be a happier, more confident you?

_____

_____

_____

_____

_____

_____

_____

_____

_____

_____

_____

_____

_____

_____

_____

_____

_____

_____

_____

_____

_____

_____

CHAPTER 7

I'm Not Loved

As humans, we all have a strong need to feel loved and be connected to others. Love is such an important emotion that it drives many of our thoughts and actions. When we feel loved and connected, life seems easier somehow. When we lack love and connection, we often feel lonely and incomplete.

"I'm not loved" often shows up as:

- Nobody likes me.
- I'm all alone in this world.
- Everybody abandoned me.
- I'm unlovable.
- Who would love me?

Case Study: Angry Jessica
Client: Jessica, Age: 16

Presenting Problem

Susan brought her daughter, Jessica, in for help because of Jessica's increasing anger outbursts in the past few months. Within the past three weeks, things have gotten significantly worse, with Jessica getting into two verbal fights and one fistfight at school. Jessica is also fighting with her younger sister daily. Susan feels hopeless and unsure of what to do. The counselor at Jessica's school recommended that she sees her doctor for medication to "calm her nerves."

Family History

Jessica lives with both parents and a younger sister. Jessica has never been close to either parent. Her older brother, Jonathon, was her best friend and idol. A drunk driver killed him when Jessica was nine years old. Her little sister, Jennifer, was born the following year. Jessica has always resented Jennifer.

Social History

Jessica is a good student who excels at math, English, and arts. She is a bit of a loner and has only one close friend and several acquaintances. While she is liked and welcomed by other people, Jessica prefers to be alone.

Jessica spends most of her time listening to music and drawing.

Words Jessica Often Heard Others Used to Describe Her

Talented, quiet, artsy, loner, nice, smart

Words Jessica Uses to Describe Herself

Artsy, creative, loner, angry, alone in this world

Session One Notes

Jessica was full of anger and frustration when she came in. She said she hated feeling this way, but she also doesn't know how to stop. She spent the first 15 minutes of the session pacing back and forth while talking to me. After doing a few relaxation exercises, she finally calms down.

Jessica expressed significant anger toward her parents. She feels the only time they paid any attention to her was when she was in trouble; otherwise, they act like she doesn't exist. Jessica hates being a part of her family. "Everyone is messed up, yet they (referring to her parents) always pretend that we're the perfect, happy family."

Jessica spent most of the session venting, rapidly firing off all the "stupid" stuff her parents did to keep their perfect, happy family front.

Her thoughts were racing, and many ideas did not connect. Jessica would break down and cry in frustration because she couldn't express herself.

We spent much of the session practicing calming techniques and allowing Jessica to vent and cry.

Session Two Notes

Jessica was much calmer today. She proudly stated that she has been doing her calming exercises, and they have been helping to take the edge off.

We spent today exploring the death of her brother and what it meant to her.

Jessica recalled that her childhood was great. Although she didn't have a close relationship with her parents, things were OK between them. She received all the love and attention she needed from her brother, Jonathon, who was also her best friend. They did everything together. Even when Jonathon's friends wanted to exclude Jessica, he would always choose her even if meant being excluded himself.

Jonathon was a wonderful artist, naturally. His drawing talents were well known at school. Jessica had always admired that about Jonathon. In the six months preceding his death, Jonathon had taken a significant interest in helping Jessica develop her drawing abilities. They would spend hours creating and perfecting their work.

Then, the nightmare happened. Jessica came home from grocery shopping with her mother to see many flashing lights from police cars in the street by their house. Her mother ran from the car, toward the house, only to be caught by a police officer who held her back. He said something to her that Jessica couldn't hear. Then Jessica heard the loudest, most terrifying scream she has ever heard and watched as her mother fell to the ground, continuing to wail loudly.

Jessica crept in for a closer look. Before another police officer could stop her, Jessica was standing beside her mother. In front of them was her brother's body on a stretcher. Jonathon's shirt was cut down the middle, exposing his chest. A man pulled a blanket up to cover his body and face. Before they fully covered him, Jessica remembered the cold stares from her brother's eyes—an image that still haunts her today. A drunk driver had hit and killed Jonathon as he was riding his bike in front of their home. Jonathon was 13 years old.

That night, family and friends gathered at the house to grieve and to give Jessica's family support. Although the house was filled with people, Jessica had never felt more alone than that night. Nothing was real to her. Everything and everyone moved in slow motion. Intellectually, she knew her brother had passed away. Emotionally, she couldn't accept it.

At one point that night, Jessica shouted at everyone to stop crying and go home. She didn't want to play this stupid game anymore. Jonathon had to be alive. Jessica ran around the house calling out for him to stop hiding and come out.

Jessica was quickly ushered to another room by her aunt. "You need to be brave and strong for your parents. You need to put on a brave face. They cannot deal with any more pain right now," she said and hugged Jessica.

For the rest of the night, Jessica sat quietly by herself, holding onto her drawing book for dear life. That was her only connection to Jonathon.

That night, Jessica was told to sleep in the living room so that her aunt and uncle could sleep in her room. Being in the living room by herself was so scary for Jessica. It was so big and cold. Jessica was all alone as everyone was upstairs.

Lying in the dark, Jessica felt:

1. Lonely: There is no one here for her.
2. Confused: Why did her brother have to die?
3. Unloved: There is no one left to love her.
4. Abandoned: How could her brother leave her?
5. Scared: Who will protect her now?
6. Burdened: She had to put on a brave face for her parents.
7. Sad: Her best friend is gone.
8. Fear: She couldn't get the memory of her brother's cold eyes out of her mind.

Jessica was surprised at how much detail she remembered and how much pain she still carried. With help, Jessica released most of the pain she had experienced that night.

Session Three and Four Notes

The first few weeks after Jonathon's death were unbearable for her. Not only did she lose her brother and best friend, it felt as if she also lost her parents as well. Her mother never left her bed—spending every day and every night crying. Her father could not deal with it and departed to a local bar to escape nightly. That left Jessica all by herself with no one to talk to. Her loneliness and feelings of being unloved amplified.

The next few months were a little better. Her mother started taking some medication to calm her nerves and could now get out of bed and lounge around the house. However, she moved slowly, and she had very little expression on her face, almost zombie-like. Her mother's doctor recommended grief counseling for the family, but her parents refused.

Her father started working from home. Although her parents were both physically there, they were emotionally checked out. The conversations they did have centered around her father's work and her mother's pills. Occasionally, they would bring up Jonathon, saying what a perfect son he was and how the house is dead now that he's gone.

Jessica remembered wanting to yell, "I'm here. I'm alive. Pay attention to me!"

Jessica became more and more withdrawn as the feelings of being unloved grew stronger in her mind. She wondered what was wrong with her. She didn't know why she was so unlovable.

Six months after Jonathon's death, her mother came back to life. She began to cook and clean again. Occasionally, she would even ask Jessica to come and watch TV with her. Her father even looked happier somehow.

Jessica was confused but didn't care. She was just happy to have some attention from her parents again.

Later that month, her parents sat her down to announce the great news. Her mom exclaimed, "Our family has been saved! We will have life in this house again!" Jessica's mom was pregnant, and they were expecting a baby in January.

Jessica was in shock. She didn't know what to say. She didn't know what to feel. "A baby? Life in this house again? I'm alive! I have always been alive! Doesn't my life count?" Jessica remembered thinking.

Fast-forward a few years later; Jessica reports feeling even more distant from her parents. They spent so much time and attention on Jennifer that they rarely noticed Jessica's presence. Sure, they pretended to include her in on their activities sometimes, but the offers were so fake that they angered Jessica even more.

Session Five Notes

Jessica reports feeling even more neglected within the last six months. Jennifer is now in first grade and her parents are spending even more time with her. This leaves little time for Jessica. Her anger and resentment have been growing stronger, and it's affecting her attitude at school and at home. Jessica feels like she has this monster inside her that just wants to come out and unleash its anger onto the world. Recently, Jessica has been unable to control herself and has gotten into several fights.

Private Session with Jessica's Parents

Both parents agreed and confirmed Jessica's story that they were emotionally unavailable the months after Jonathon's death. They felt bad about it and tried to make it up to Jessica. However, most of the time, their efforts were shot down or ignored. Jessica would often tell them, "I'm doing fine. I like being by myself." They thought the best they could do for her was to allow her to be herself as she dealt with her grief in her own way.

This pattern persisted for years to come. Jessica was always by herself, doing her own thing. Her mother said, "She was such a good student and never complained about anything. We thought she was just an introvert... a loner. Every time we asked her to do something with us, she would say 'no.' We didn't want to force anything on her."

Jessica agreed with this story but added that she felt the invitations were never sincere. Jessica insisted that if they loved her, they would understand her better.

Session Six to Twelve Notes

The next few sessions were spent working with Jessica and her parents individually to help them process the pain of Jonathon's death and the rift in their relationships. Jessica could finally let go of her anger toward her parents and work through her grief of losing her brother. She also let go of the resentment toward Jennifer.

Three-Month Follow-Up

Jessica and her parents' relationship is improving steadily. Jessica can now see that they do love her and value her as a family member. Jessica also saw how her actions played a role in her feeling unloved. Her lack of willingness to take part in family activities and her constantly telling them she enjoyed being by herself caused a lot of misunderstanding and pain. Jessica learned that she needed to be an active participant in creating the life she wanted. Jessica also reports that she's getting along better with Jennifer.

Six-Month Follow-Up

Jessica joined the art club at school and now has several close friends. She reports being much happier with life. The anger is no longer present. Jessica feels at peace. Her relationship with her parents and Jennifer is still improving. In fact, Jessica is now teaching Jennifer how to draw.

Lesson Learned

This is a strong lesson in how you create your own reality. Because of Jonathon's death and the subsequent months afterward, Jessica learned to believe that she was not loved. Lost in their pain, Jessica's parents left her alone, causing her to feel alone, lonely and unlovable.

Once Jessica believed that she was unloved, her subconscious mind went into high gear, looking for evidence to support her beliefs. Every time her parents weren't paying attention to her was another piece of evidence to validate her beliefs. When her parents attempted to connect with her, Jessica refused.

Jessica's belief that she was not loved, and that she was unlovable made it impossible for her to see that these were loving actions directed toward her. Rather, she thought they were fake attempts, and she became lonelier and angrier.

Jessica's experience is a great example of why professional help is important after trauma. The family could have grieved together and possibly become closer, rather than falling apart. Further, Jessica might also have an easier time accepting Jennifer from the start if Jessica felt safe and secure in her relationship with her parents.

REMEMBER: Whether you spend your time and energy focusing on the negatives or the positives of any situation, you will spend your time and energy in some way. Why not focus on the positive aspects rather than the negatives and create happy experiences for yourself? You deserve to be happy and you are in charge of your happiness.

Self-Reflection

What is your biggest take-away from this chapter?

_____

_____

_____

_____

_____

_____

_____

_____

_____

_____

_____

_____

_____

_____

_____

_____

_____

_____

_____

_____

How can you use what you've just learned to take charge of your mind and be a happier, more confident you?

_____

_____

_____

_____

_____

_____

_____

_____

_____

_____

_____

_____

_____

_____

_____

_____

_____

_____

_____

_____

_____

CHAPTER 8

I'm Not Safe

I'm not safe can refer to both physical safety and emotional safety and often shows up as:

- People want to hurt me physically or emotionally.
- I'm too weak to defend myself.
- People are evil.
- People take advantage of me.
- The world is so scary.
- It's me against the world.

Case Study: Helpless Hailey
Client: Hailey   Age: 13

Presenting Problem

Hailey was brought in by her mother, Pamela, because

she has become increasingly fearful of being alone. Hailey normally sleeps with her door closed and her lights off. One day, for no apparent reason, Hailey had a very rough, sleepless night. From that night on, she had to keep the door open and the lights on when she went to bed. Over the next few months, she became more anxious and afraid.

Hailey's anxiety and fear of being alone are so high that she cannot be by herself for more than 10-15 minutes without going into an anxious state that requires her mother's intervention. She constantly follows her mother and her fifteen-year-old brother, Jack, around the house. Recently, Hailey started begging to sleep in her mom's room. Her brother is resentful because he lost a significant amount of freedom as he now has to "babysit" her.

Family History

Hailey is the youngest of two siblings being raised by a single mom. Hailey's father passed away from cancer when she was an infant. Both Hailey and her brother were too young to understand the impact at the time of their father's death. Pamela has never remarried and is a devoted mother.

Social History

Hailey is a "B" student with many close friends at school and church. She gets along well with her peers and adults. She has been attending the same church weekly for many years and until four months ago, was highly active in her church's youth group. Now, Hailey prefers to be home with her family.

Words Hailey Often Heard Others Used to Describe Her

Nice, helpful, friendly, funny, outgoing, cheerful

Words Hailey Uses to Describe Herself

Average, anxious, scared all the time, afraid to be alone, childish, something is wrong with me

Session One Notes

Hailey is a sweet girl with a ready smile and a soft voice. She was a little nervous at first but warmed up easily. She stated, "I'm will do what you tell me because I'm tired of being scared."

Hailey denied any abuse, trauma, or significant events in her life. She reported no use of alcohol or drugs.

Hailey is confused and frustrated because she can't understand why this is happening. She feels tired of being scared and wants to go back to her normal life. Life was good for Hailey until four months ago when she could not sleep one night. As Hailey tossed and turned in her bed, she saw what she thought were shadows moving along her walls. She didn't think much of it at first because she knew she was tired. She figured her eyes were playing tricks on her.

As the night progressed, Hailey would go in and out of sleep. Each time she woke up, she would become more and more anxious and the shadow movements became more and more pronounced.

At one point, Hailey was certain there was someone in her room. She grabbed her cell phone and used the flashlight function to check her room and made sure no one was there.

The next night, Hailey had difficulty falling asleep again. However, this time, Hailey felt anxious immediately and had to open her door and turn her lights on for comfort. This started Hailey's new pattern of sleeping with her door open and her lights on.

A few weeks later, Hailey was studying in her room as she has always done before. Her mother was making dinner downstairs and her brother was in the living room, watching TV. Again, for no apparent reason, Hailey felt significant anxiety and fear that something was wrong. She ran downstairs to check on her mother and brother. For the rest of the night, Hailey stayed close to her mother.

Hailey started spending less and less time alone. At first, Pamela liked the company and was enjoying this increased mother daughter bonding experience. She didn't realize there was a problem until Jack brought it up at dinner one night. Jack told Pamela he was sick and tired of Hailey always following him around. He felt he didn't have any freedom because everywhere he was, Hailey was right there by his side. He felt suffocated. He demanded that it stop.

For the first time, Pamela realized that this bonding experience was, in fact, Hailey being very clingy.

Looking back, Pamela realized that Hailey never spent time alone anymore, except for bedtime. Pamela also never thought much about Hailey's new sleeping preference, but in retrospect, everything became clearer.

To help Hailey, Pamela started becoming firmer, insisting Hailey practice spending some time alone each day. Each time Hailey tried to spend time alone, it only lasted about fifteen minutes. She would then run to Pamela, crying and hyperventilating. Pamela had to help guide her with deep breathing exercises to calm her down.

When Hailey started begging to sleep with her mother, Pamela finally realized the severity of the problem and sought help.

Although there were no real significant events that caused Hailey to experience that first sleepless night, that night was so traumatic for her. In those in-between sleep states, Hailey felt very anxious and unsafe.

Because this event was so significant and so specific, we were able to use a simple method to scramble this movie in her mind. At the end of the session, Hailey left feeling more confident in herself.

The next morning, Pamela called to tell me that Hailey slept with only a night light on. She went to bed feeling a little nervous, but very excited to see if the session helped. This was Hailey's first night of rested sleep in a long time.

Session Two Notes

The following week, Hailey came back with a lot of eagerness to continue our work together. She reported that she has been able to sleep with the lights off for the last three nights. However, she was still afraid to be by herself and still spent much of her time following her mom and brother around. We spent the rest of the session working on changing her mindset to accept that she is courageous and safe.

Root Cause

During session three, we discovered an incident that happened when Hailey was three years old. Hailey went to play in the backyard by herself. She has done this many time before.

However, when she came back into the house this time, she could not find her mother or brother. She called out for them and searched the whole house. She was terrified because she couldn't find them. In that instance, Hailey was certain that someone had come in and kidnapped them. She was afraid she would never see them again.

Hailey recalled feeling extremely alone and terrified that the people who kidnapped her mother and brother would come back for her. She remembered being too scared to cry or move. Every single noise she heard, she believed to be the kidnapper coming back for her.

The next thing she remembered, Hailey woke up in the dark, in her own bed, with a lot of pain to her forehead. She screamed out for her mom and her mom came running to her.

Hailey later found out that her mother and brother had just stepped outside of their house to say "hi" to the new neighbors. Hailey's mom saw she was enjoying playing in the backyard and didn't want to interrupt her.

When her mom came back inside the house, she found Hailey sleeping by the stairs and brought her to her bed. Evidently, she must have passed out in fear and hit her head, but her mom was unaware. She just thought Hailey fell asleep while waiting for them to come in and took her to bed.

Because the event was so significant and so specific, we were able to scramble it easily. Hailey was able to see the full picture and accepted that she was safe, and her mother and brother were also safe the whole time.

Once Hailey fully understood and accepted the reality of the situation, she was able to move on.

Three-Month Follow-Up

Life has returned to normal for Hailey and her family. Hailey reported being able to sleep with the lights off and be comfortable by herself. When the old fear tried to come back, she would close her eyes and imagine that she was watching an unpleasant movie and turn it off.

Occasionally, she would imagine herself turning off the old movie and switching to her favorite TV show. That brought her peace and calmness immediately. Using this simple technique has helped Hailey to take control of her life. She is now actively engaging in her youth group even more.

Hailey's mom reported an interesting side note: Haley's motivation and focus have increased significantly. She is now getting four "A's" and two "B's" in her classes at school.

Lesson Learned

This is a powerful lesson in what our minds can do to hold us hostage. While Hailey experienced no "real" trauma, her imagination and misguided beliefs when she was a toddler created a deep-rooted belief that she was not safe.

Once that belief was created and placed in her IC, it ran in the background, collecting evidence to support it. I'm certain there were many smaller incidences that validated that belief for Hailey, but the night when she couldn't sleep definitely brought this old, hidden belief to the forefront of Hailey's subconscious mind. The Stranger Danger Protocol was on high alert and Hailey experienced significant fear throughout her day. She had to stay by her mom's side for safety.

Once the emotions attached to this belief were neutralized, Hailey was able to realize and accept that she and her loved ones were safe. The Stranger Danger Protocol was turned off and Hailey was once again at peace.

REMEMBER: Your subconscious mind does not know how to differentiate between what's real and what's vividly imagined. To your subconscious mind, it's the same.

In Hailey's case, her vivid imagination at age three caused her significant pain and grief later on in her life.

Be kind to yourself. If you catch yourself creating scary what-if scenarios in your head or replaying painful experiences of your past, tell yourself to stop. Give yourself permission to focus on something different. Whatever you focus on becomes bigger. Why not focus on the things that bring you happiness?

I hope this book and the four case studies in this book helped you to understand how powerful your mind is and how you can play a significant role in creating your life experiences.

REMEMBER: You are the boss of your mind. It is up to you to give your assistant the commands that bring you closer and closer to your goals and dreams.

If you find yourself drifting away from your goals or dreams, pause, re-evaluate, and re-decide on a course of action that best serves your needs. You can learn to take control of your feelings, thoughts, and actions. You can learn to take control of your life.

Self-Reflection

What is your biggest take-away from this chapter?

_____

_____

_____

_____

_____

_____

_____

_____

_____

_____

_____

_____

_____

_____

_____

_____

_____

_____

_____

_____

_____

How can you use what you've just learned to take charge of your mind and be a happier, more confident you?

_____

_____

_____

_____

_____

_____

_____

_____

_____

_____

_____

_____

_____

_____

_____

_____

_____

_____

_____

_____

_____

_____

5 Simple Steps to Manage Your Mood

A re you frustrated because one bad event can ruin your entire day or maybe even your entire week? Does it seem like no matter what you try to do, you just can't seem to shake those negative thoughts and feelings? Instead of being able to let go of things easily, do you often hang on to things long after everyone else seems to have forgotten about them?

If you answered "yes" to these questions, you are not alone. Many people have a hard time letting things go. Instead, when something goes wrong, they replay that scenario constantly in their head, causing them to feel worse about themselves or worse about the other person or people involved.

Think about the last argument you had with someone that bothered you. What was that like? Did you replay the argument repeatedly and beating yourself up for all the things you wished you had done or said differently? Did you make up conversations that didn't even take place and feeling even more upset? Did you think about other similar situations and spiraling downward into sadness, anger, or pain?

Let's say that after the argument had taken place, you wanted to patch things up. Were you able to shake those negativities so you could do what you wanted to do, or were you weighed down and held back by your emotions? Did you feel in control of your emotions or did you feel as if your emotions were controlling you?

For many people, shaking those negative feelings is difficult even when they want to let things go. This is because they don't understand just how much power and control, they *do* have over their emotions. Maybe this is where you are right now.

Understanding your feelings and knowing what to do about them may seem like a difficult and overwhelming task right now. However, with the right tools, this task can become manageable and even easy. When you use the following 5 simple questions to guide you, you can understand and release your unwanted feelings easily so you can focus on rebuilding or strengthening your relationships and reclaiming your happiness.

You can use these same 5 simple questions to help you regain your happiness whether your disagreement is with a parent, a friend, or even with yourself.

Available in paperback, eBook and audiobook (and Companion Journal)

Jump Start Your Confidence and Boost Your Self-Esteem

Do you often feel as though other people are better than you? Does it seem they are more carefree, more outgoing, and more confident? They make friends easily and good things seem to happen for them all the time. They are fun, witty, and full of charm. Everywhere they go, people are drawn to them. They do what they want and say what they think.

These positive, likable traits seem to come so naturally for them. But for you, life is filled with anxiety, fear, and self-doubt. What is their secret? How can they talk to anyone about anything with ease, while it's a significant struggle for you to just be in the presence of others, let alone carry on a conversation?

You dream of being different. You dream of being comfortable in your own skin. You dream of creating meaningful relationships, going after what you want with confidence, and feeling happy and satisfied with your everyday life. But your fear and self-doubt may be holding you back, causing you to feel trapped and powerless to change your situation. You're left feeling sad, lonely, and insecure about yourself and your life.

What if there was a way to change all of that? What if you could destroy your fear and self-doubt and be strong and self-assured instead? What would it be like if you could go into any situation with excitement, courage, and confidence? Imagine what your life would look like and what you could achieve. Just imagine.

I'm will let you in on a little secret. That excitement, courage, and confidence which you admire in others are skills you can learn.

Sure, there are some people for whom these traits come naturally, but if you were not born with these traits, you can learn them. The thing is, you can learn to change your negative thinking, destroy your fear and self-doubt, and go after whatever you want with confidence. You can learn to be comfortable in your own skin and be completely at ease while expressing yourself.

You were born with incredible powers within yourself – powers I like to refer to as, Inner Superpowers (ISPs). When tapped into, these ISPs will help you be happy, resilient, and successful in life. The problem is that you have not been aware of these ISPs, nor how to use them.

Maybe you saw a glimpse of them here and there, but you didn't recognize their power or have faith in them. If you don't know what your Inner Superpowers are, how can you tap into them consistently and achieve the results you want and deserve?

In this book, you will learn:

- The seven Inner Superpowers guaranteed to destroy your fear and self-doubt
- Create a strong sense of self-esteem and unshakable confidence.
- Easy to use tools to change your negative thinking into empowering thoughts
- How to connect to and strengthen your Inner Superpowers
- How to consistently tap into and unleash your Inner Superpowers whenever you want to
- How to live within your full power and be happy, confident, and successful in life—and more!

You have so many Inner Superpowers that make you wonderful in every way. In this book, I have chosen to share seven specific ISPs because these seven are your best bet for destroying fear and self-doubt.

There is much written about each of these ISPs and each ISPs can be a stand-alone book. However, I know your time is valuable and you have other responsibilities and activities to tend to. This is why you'll find that these chapters are brief and to the point.

Available in paperback, eBook and audiobook

About the Author

Dear Reader,

If you are a teenager struggling with high stress, anxiety, self-doubt, low-confidence or depressive symptoms, I want you to know that you are not alone. I know because I have been there myself. My name is Jacqui Letran, and I have over eighteen years of experience helping thousands of teens, and I know I can help you!

I know you're frustrated, scared, and lonely. I was too. I also know confidence, success, and happiness are achievable because I have successfully freed myself from those old emotions and embraced my life with excitement, confidence, and joy. My goal is to help you understand the power of your mind and show you how you can master it to overcome your struggles and step into the magnificence of your own being, just like I did—and just like thousands of others have done using these same techniques.

Who am I and why I care.

My life was rather easy and carefree until I hit my teenage years. Overnight, all my friends transformed from girls into women! They began to wear makeup and dressed in expensive and sexy clothes. They flirted with boys. Some even flaunted the older boys they were dating in front me. I, on the other hand, remained trapped in my boyish body. And, within the rules of my superstrict mother, wearing makeup, sexy clothes, or going on dates were not options for me.

I felt different and isolated—and I quickly lost all my friends. I didn't know what to say or how to act around others. I felt awkward and left behind as if I didn't belong anywhere. I just didn't fit in anymore. I became more and more withdrawn as I wondered what was wrong with me. Why didn't I blossom into a woman like all my friends? Why was life so difficult and so unfair?

- I blamed my mother for my problems. "If she weren't so strict, she would allow me to date and have nice, sexy clothes," I thought. At least then I would fit in, and everything would be perfect!
- I also felt very angry. My life had taken a turn for the worst—but no one seemed to care or even notice. I started skipping school, began smoking, and getting into fights. I walked around with a chip on my shoulder and an "I don't care" attitude
- I felt invisible, unimportant, and unworthy. Deep down, I only wanted to be accepted as I was. I wanted to belong. I wanted to be loved

I thought my wishes were answered when I was sixteen. I meet a man five years older than me. He showered his love and affection on me and made me feel as if I was the most important person on earth. Six months later, I was a high school dropout, pregnant teen living on public assistance. I felt more alienated than ever before. Everywhere I went, I felt judged and looked down upon. I felt despair and was certain my life was over. I had no future. I knew I was destined to live a miserable life.

I felt truly alone in the world.

Except I wasn't alone; I had a baby growing inside of me. The day I gave birth to my son and saw his angelic face, I knew that it was up to me to break this cycle of self-destructive thoughts and actions.

That's when everything changed!

I began to read every self-help book I could get my hands on. I was on a mission of self-discovery and self-love. I began to let go of the old beliefs that prevented me from seeing myself as capable, intelligent, and beautiful.

The more I let go of those old beliefs, the more confident I became and the more I accomplished. It was a powerful lesson in how changing my thoughts resulted in changing my life.

Six years later, at twenty-three, I earned my master's degree in nursing and became a Nurse Practitioner. Since then, I have dedicated over eighteen years of my life working in adolescent health. I love using my gift and passion to empower teens to create a bright future for themselves.

As I reflect on my painful teen years, I realize how I played a major role in determining my life experiences. My low confidence had paralyzed me from taking action, thus reinforcing my misguided belief that I was different or inferior.

I knew I had to share this knowledge to help teens avoid some of the pain I had experienced.

In my eighteen-plus year career specializing in Adolescent Health, I have:

- Established, owned and operated Teen Confidence Academy, specializing in helping teens overcome stress, anxiety, and depressive symptoms without medication or long-term traditional therapy,

- Established, owned and operated multiple "Teen Choice Medical Center" locations,
- Become a Speaker, Podcaster, and Multi Award-Winning Author,
- Educated and supported thousands of teens and adults to overcome stress, anxiety and depressive symptoms,
- Raised a loving, intelligent, and confident man (he is my pride and joy), and
- Completed post-graduate training in holistic and alternative health and healing methods.

I am deeply passionate about helping teens let go of their barriers so they can see the beauty and greatness with-in themselves. I believe each of us deserves a life full of health, love, and happiness. I also believe that every person has within them all the resources needed to achieve a beautiful and fulfilling life.

In my younger days, when I was going through my troubled teen years, I needed a place where I could be mentored, where I could learn, reflect, and grow; a place where I could heal and get a proper, healthy perspective of myself, and the world around me. I didn't have that option then, or at least I didn't know where to find it.

That is why I became a Mindset Mentor specializing in teen confidence, and that's why I am writing this book for you now.

Thousands of teens are living in quiet desperation right now because no one has shown them the key to their success. My goal in writing this book is to teach you about your mind so you can control your thoughts, feelings, and actions. You can take charge of creating the life that you want and deserve. You deserve to be successful and happy in life. Let's make it happen!

Jacqui Letran

With Gratitude

Among the many people who have helped make this book possible, I would like to express my sincere and heartfelt thanks to my best friend and husband, Joseph Wolfgram. Without his love and support, this book would not have been possible. Thank you for always encouraging me, supporting me, and seeing the greatness within me before I can see it myself. Thank you for being my rock.

To Alan Letran, who is my loving son, my inspiration, and my wonderful life teacher. It is true what they say, "Children raise their parents." He has taught me countless invaluable lessons about my life and myself, and I will be eternally grateful. He is and will always be the greatest love of my life.

To all of my teachers and mentors, whether in a professional relationship or in life experiences, a big thank you for being a part of my life. Your presence in my life has helped me grow and transform from a scared little girl into a confident, healthy, and happy woman.

I would like to express a very special thank you to my most inspirational mentor, Robin Duncan, of the Miracle Center of California. Under her guidance, I've deepened my learning about the major negative core beliefs that cause most people their pain, and how to lovingly help my clients to overcome them.

Connect with Me

I love hearing from my readers; please feel free to connect with me at my Amazon page:

Amazon.com/author/JacquiLetran

-or-

JacquiLetran.com

Facebook.com/JacquiLetran

Linkedin.com/in/JacquiLetran

Instagram.com/JacquiLetran

You can also contact me at:

Author@JacquiLetran.com

Free Book Club Visits

If your book club reads any of the Words of Wisdom for Teens Series, I would love to attend your club's meeting virtually to answer questions you or your members might have.

You can book your free 30-minute spot by emailing me at **Author@JacquiLetran.com**   Put "Free Book Club Visit" in the subject line.

Words of Wisdom for Teens Series
Award-Winning Guides for Teen Girls

5 Simple Steps to Manage your Mood
A Guide for Teen Girls: How to Let Go of Negative Feelings and Create a Happy Relationship with Yourself and Others

5 Simple Steps to Manage your Mood Journal
A Companion Journal to Help You Track, Understand and Take Charge of Your Mood

I would, but my DAMN MIND won't let me
A Guide for Teen Girls: How to understand and control your thoughts and feelings

Jump Start Your Confidence and Boost Your Self-Esteem
A Guide for Teen Girls Unleash Your Inner Superpowers to Conquer Fear and Self-Doubt and Build Unshakable Confidence,

Stop the Bully Within Podcast

After seeing thousands of clients, I noticed a common theme among most of those I help—they are their own biggest bully.

Just pause for a moment and think of the words you say to yourself when you did something wrong or failed at something. Are those loving and supportive words? Would you say those same words to someone you love?

For many people, when they think of a bully, they think of someone outside of them—someone who says and does mean things to cause others pain. Not too many people think about the bully they have within themselves.

I'm on a mission to bring awareness to how damaging this "bully within" can be, and to help people learn how to transform that inner critic into their best friend, cheerleader, and personal champion for success.

Listen to the Podcast at
StoptheBullyWithin.com

Made in the USA
Middletown, DE
21 January 2021